The Light of Advent

Gospel Readings & Reflections

Bishop Daniel E. Flores

CDOB Communications

San Juan, Texas

2020

CDOB Communications
700 N. Virgen de San Juan Blvd.
San Juan, Texas 78589

©2020 CDOB Communications
All rights reserved.
ISBN-10: 1-7359840-0-1
ISBN-13: 978-1-7359840-0-1

Cover art: *Annunciazione* by Garofalo (Benvenuto Tisi), 1528,
Musei Capitolini in Rome.
Cover design by Rick Treviño

Table of Contents

Daily Gospel Responses & Questions
Provided by

Week 1   *pages 23 - 38*
Sister Fatima Santiago
Missionary Sister of the Immaculate Heart of Mary
with Proyecto Desarrollo Humano in Peñitas

Week 2   *pages 47-54, 60-67*
Deacon Josh Ramirez
Holy Family Parish in Brownsville

Week 3   *pages 83-102*
Lydia Pesina
Director, Family Life Office, Diocese of Brownsville

Week 4   *pages 112-123*
Father Andrés Gutiérrez
Pastor at Holy Spirit Parish in McAllen

Mens Mariae

Verbum habitavit in mentem Mariae
prius quam ad ventrem appropinquavit,
sed in carne Verbum gestis movet
ut in mentem nostram germinetur.

La Mente de María

El Verbo moraba en la mente de María
antes de acercarse a su vientre,
pero por nosotros en carne se mueve
para acercarse a nuestra mente.

Mary's Mind

The WORD in Mary's mind did dwell
before to her womb he drew near
but for us he moves in flesh
that to the WORD we might rise and see clear.

The Annunciation

Introduction

The WORD Accompanies Us

The Gospel of the first Sunday of Advent tells us we should be about preparing for the Christ who comes in Glory at the end of time, when he will manifest the fullness of his redemptive work. The first Sunday of Advent is not only about preparing for the days of Christmas, for it also opens for us the whole liturgical year. The liturgical year is oriented in such a way that it allows us to enter into the grace of the first coming of Christ, the mysteries of his life, death and resurrection to prepare us for the second coming. Why do we celebrate Christmas, or any major liturgical feast? Very simply, we celebrate the birth of Christ and the feasts associated to his coming into the world so as to enter and participate in the grace of the Christ that we need now, at this time, as he prepares us for his final coming in glory.

It is in this spirit of *the grace once given, the grace now present, the grace that is to be fulfilled* that this little book of Advent reflections is offered.

Advent can pass too quickly. It takes an effort on our part as members of the Church to savor the time Advent offers us as we prepare for Christmas and as we orient ourselves towards the mysteries of the entire liturgical year. Only with great effort do our daily lives make time available to the Lord so he can speak to us and touch us interiorly. But we must try, so that he can orient us by faith, hope and charity towards the horizon of an eternity that draws near to us.

When people ask me what I recommend for their spiritual lives, for their lives of daily prayer, I usually say that whatever else we do in our spiritual lives, the tradition of the Church teaches us that we should all be reading the Scriptures and thinking about them. Let the words enter your mind, I say, and respond to them, because they are the living words of Christ to the Church, and to each one of us. I think the easiest way to do this, and perhaps the most efficacious, is to make time to meditate on the daily Gospel readings of the Mass. But it is not enough to read and think; we must respond to the Lord. He gives us a Word, and we are blessed to be able to give him a word of love in return.

The most basic element of a Catholic life is knowing, loving and following the person of Christ Jesus Our Lord. All of our spirituality flows from this, and to this knowing, loving and following. The entire sacramental life of the Church aims towards this. The Sacred Scriptures, as the words of the WORD propel us towards this. The words of the WORD are lived in the Church in her daily liturgies. The Liturgy of the Hours, and the daily readings appointed for the celebrations of daily Mass accompany us and form us, if we let them. Through them the Lord himself accompanies and forms us. We must let him, through his words and the things he does, sink into our minds, our hearts, and we must let him move our wills to active living by charity of what we have heard.

Jesus in the Gospels engaged the people around him; he taught, he asked questions, he performed signs, he engaged in controversies with the leadership. Throughout it all, he invited, sought and intentionally provoked a response from his hearers. Sometimes they asked questions: "Lord, what must I do to be saved?" Sometimes he inspired awe: "Depart from me Lord, for I am a sinner." Sometimes he engaged intense personal dialogues: "But, Lord, even the puppies eat the scraps from the master's table." So it can and should be for us.

Prayer is both a habit and a grace. I usually pray early in the morning, and in addition to the Liturgy of the Hours and the Rosary, my prayer always includes time to hear what the Lord says to the Church in the Gospel of the Day. I try to respond to it within myself. Some kind of response to this morning-time with the Liturgy, the Rosary and the Readings is what I post most mornings on my Twitter feed. I think that if the Lord grants me a grace to hear and respond to him in some small way, I should try to offer an expression of that to others. I want to encourage others to have daily engagement with the Lord in the Gospel, and in this way let him, by the Holy Spirit, form our minds, hearts and wills. This, I think, is the most important thing we should all be doing.

This Advent book in a way flows out of my own daily habit of engaging the Scriptures. So the book consists, first of all, of the daily Gospel for each of the days of Advent, including the major Marian Feast Days.

It also includes a collection of things I have written over the years during my time as bishop of the Diocese of Brownsville. They are writings focused on this great season of preparation and anticipation. The book also contains a few verses I have written over time, and some sacred art that I occasionally meditate on. I am neither a poet nor an artist, though I enjoy the company of words and am provoked sometimes to meditation by sacred art. Both encourage me in my interior life. The art speaks for itself, which is why it is art.

I think, for example, of the images of the Annunciation. Artists have since early medieval times shown Mary with a book in front of her, as an indication that she was meditating on the Scriptures when the Angel came to her. She is the woman of the Word; she meditated it, lived it, and was able to respond with her gracious "yes" when she was asked to welcome the WORD in her soul also into her flesh. The responsiveness of Mary, a responsiveness full of grace and always flowing from grace, is the preeminent paradigm for the Church, and the model for our prayer with the Word.

Some of the verses I have written are in English, and some in Spanish. Most are translated. It's anyone's guess which came first, the Spanish or the English. Two of the poems on these pages are in Spanish only. That is because we respond to God in the languages that we commonly hear and speak. As many of you know, here in the Rio Grande Valley, when I preach I often shift from English and Spanish; it is fairly connatural to me, and I don't always translate what I say. Such is the case with some of the verses in this volume.

My own responses over the years to the daily Gospel readings from the Lectionary as posted on my Twitter feed are interspersed in this book with the Gospel readings for the day. I do not intend these to dominate the conversation, but rather to spur the conversations of others with the Lord himself. That is why I invited four people – Sister Fatima Santiago, a Missionary Sister of the Immaculate Heart of Mary (ICM), with *Proyecto Desarrollo Humano* in Peñitas; Lydia Pesina from our Family Life Office; Deacon Josh Ramirez from Holy Family Church in Brownsville; and Father Andy Gutiérrez from Holy Spirit Church in McAllen – to offer their own responses by way of a few lines for each of the daily Gospel readings for the different weeks of Advent. I am grateful they each accepted the invitation. Their participation is a great gift that shows us that we respond to the Lord out of the grace that is given to each one of us in our uniqueness, and in the varieties of our daily living, our varied vocations, and our human experiences.

It is my hope that their own responses to what the Lord says in the Gospel, together with mine, will help prompt you the reader to respond to God's Word in some way. This is the heart of the matter, for I am convinced that the quality of our Christian life and witness depends on our daily engagement with the words the Lord has spoken to us. Thus, in addition to the daily Gospel readings for the days of Advent, the book contains space for your own response and reflections. Scripture is always inviting us to respond to what God says and does.

During this time when the pandemic affects our every step, when the future of our world, our country, and our families worry and preoccupy us, at a time when even Catholics seem to forget how to love one another, and instead look for better ways to argue with one another, let us all commit ourselves to a good Advent; let us commit ourselves first of all to hearing the words and deeds of Jesus and responding to them, so that they can change us into the courageous bearers of hope and charity that the Lord desires us to be. If we seek these things first, as Christ in us increases, our fears and resentments diminish. If we seek Christ first, all other things will be added besides.

I offer this little aid to Advent prayer in gratitude to the Most Holy Trinity, and to the Blessed Virgin Mary, Mother of God. I offer it also with much love for the people of the Rio Grande Valley. My life is greatly blessed for living among a people so generous and good. From them I learn how to be a better follower of Christ.

The Sundays and Feasts of Advent

On the Solemnity of Our Lord Jesus Christ, King of the Universe, which we celebrate the last Sunday of the liturgical year, I joked at one of the Masses that I think people sometimes fear that their time for shopping is nearing the end more than they fear the Final Judgment. We learn a lot about what we love by examining what we fear. The Gospel of the Solemnity of Christ the King guides us to that essential truth that Christ will come in glory. Do we love him enough to fear losing him?

The first Sunday of Advent also presents us with the person of Christ who comes in the clouds at the end of time, as the Creed tells us: he will come again to judge the living and the dead. God gives us time to get some perspective on where we are going and the goal of our Christian life. Indeed, the First Sunday of Advent pushes us to consider time: the gift of it, the purposes of it, the unstoppable movement of it.

Our age tends to live in the present moment, which is not a bad thing, since that is the only moment we have to live. The problem is trying to live in the present moment as if the past were not with us, and as if the future is the uncontrollable set of circumstances we don't know about yet. The pandemic has made us fear the future more than we used to, because we are more aware that there are many things we cannot control. We are more afraid, though we do not like to admit it.

+++

All the more reason for us to consider the person of Christ coming in his glory to judge the living and the dead. Time may not be under our control, but it remains in his. All time, says the Church at the Easter Vigil, belongs to him. Do we know him in whom we have trusted? Love is the only remedy for fear. The love of God is shown to us because God the Son came down from heaven and was born of the Virgin Mary. Further, he died for us while we were yet sinners, and rose again in fulfillment of the Scriptures.

This is precisely the reason why the Church has a calendar: It is a way of representing the mysteries of our salvation. It is the grace of the past given to the present, orienting us towards the second coming of Christ. The present remembers the love of God, and this is behind everything we celebrate. The Church's liturgical memory is the way God's life and love flows into our present and prepares our future. In our graced beginning is the seed of our graced end; in the present is the graced hope of our future.

Later in the second and third Sundays of Advent, one of the things we see is how the preaching of John the Baptist is so important to the Church. John the Baptist has a vital part in the preparation for Christmas because he, as an adult, preaches and announces or prepares the way for Christ the adult. The Church understands that we are always in a position of waiting for the coming of Christ, and that always requires repentance. Further, the justice John the Baptist preached is always a present call. John the Baptist is the great preacher of these two things, repentance and justice.

As we prepare for the birth of Christ and that celebration, the call to repentance is something we have to take seriously. Sin entangles us; and only by the grace of God, by his redemption, by his coming into the world, can we be liberated. We are preparing for the coming of Christ at Christmas, but we are also preparing for the coming of Christ at the end of time. In this way, the liturgical year is telling us that we are always waiting and require a grace that God gives us, a grace of repentance and a grace of alertness, and a love for justice.

+++

As we draw closer to the celebration of Christmas on the 25th, we focus more intently on the coming of Christ at his birth. Normally, the fourth Sunday of Advent focuses our memory on the angel appearing to the Blessed Mother, or of his talking to St. Joseph in his dreams. God was preparing them, and at the same time they were prepared to receive him when he came. This is how grace works. Christ prepares his own path. We are being prepared. In the long run, we are always preparing for the coming of Christ from now on and until his coming to the end of time. Each moment along the way has its grace attached.

It is a beautiful mystery that in the middle of the four Sundays of Advent we always celebrate two of the most essential Marian feasts of the Church, especially in South Texas and for the Americas: the Solemnity of the Immaculate Conception and the Feast of the Virgin of Guadalupe. In her Immaculate Conception, Mary is the preeminent sign that God prepares his own coming into the world. He chose Mary to be the Mother of his Son in the very act of preparing her, preserving her from any stain of sin. It is pure grace. Likewise, in the mystery of Guadalupe, there is the pure grace of the Virgin sent as a sign of Christ's desire to be born in the Americas. Again, it is a call to repentance, it is a call to preparation, it is a call to welcome Christ who never comes without the tender assistance he himself sought from the Blessed Virgin.

+++

Everything we do in the Christian life is a response to God's initiative, to his gift of himself to us. During this Advent season, we should also remember that it is this love we receive that motivates us to give something in return. It was love that motivated God the Father to give us his Son, the great gift. It was the love that motivated the Blessed Virgin, inspired by the Holy Spirit, to give us her Son. The son of Mary is the Son of the Father. Christ is the great gift.

If we see the reason, the root of the gift, perhaps it would help us to understand why we might get the panic of buying things. Don't panic. Our life is not about buying things, it is about giving things. If we could focus on that, the mystery of Christ, who is the great gift, it can keep us focused on the reason we want to give. Every moment is a gift from God. It is not something deserved. It is something that God in his generosity gives us. Each moment is a way to share that love with those around us.

Remember the widow in the Gospel, the woman who gave everything she had. The world tends to judge us by what we have, while God judges us for what we give. And this is how Advent appears. The person who knows how to live and lose his life, the one who knows how to give, will be the one who lives abundantly the grace of the kingdom. This is the way Advent prepares us for the birth of Christ.

The Church in her tradition is firmly committed to the notion that each time has its special grace. Advent is the time to focus on the gift that God prepares for our hearts. Be receptive to the generous inclinations he puts there. Let him prepare you, and you will be prepared.

Advent

Week One

The Light of Advent

"To you, O Lord, I lift up my soul ... no one who hopes in you is put to shame." (Psalm 25: 1, 3)

With these words taken from Psalm 25, the Church sings the entrance song for the Holy Eucharist the first Sunday of Advent. In some sense, the text states the main theme for the entire liturgical year. In particular, these words direct us to the main theme of the Advent season. It all has to do with the lively hope that God desires to instill within our hearts.

The theme for the whole year: We travel the paths of life, and the key questions of life arise from this reality. How should we walk, and where are we going? Sometimes the path is dark and there are no signs to guide us. Sometimes the path gets difficult and we find obstacles. There is no lack of such obstacles in our days. The economic crisis affects our best hopes for our children; the aggressiveness of the evils that afflict our communities, such as, for example, drugs and violence, continue to threaten us on all sides; the lack of respect for human rights cruelly affects the most innocent. Sometimes even Christians experience a profound discouragement, as if we were in danger of losing our hope.

The liturgy of the Holy Church offers us the light of Advent for the whole year, and for our entire lifetimes. *To you, Lord, I lift my soul.* God does not forget his people; the almighty and merciful God invites us to lift our souls to him. This means that we should walk the joys and the sorrows of life in communion with him. We must not rely just on our own strength. God hears us. But do we truly seek for his support?

God himself inspires the psalmist, and us, with the desire to lift up our souls. The soul is made capable of receiving this support in the very act of asking God for it. How, then, should we walk the path of life? We walk in life with our eyes fixed on the God who made heaven and earth. It is the Lord who inspires the good deeds we seek to do, and he directs the course of time. He encourages us with spirit of fortitude and generosity to walk our life's path.

Message for the entire Advent season: Contemplating how God has drawn near to his people, we realize that we do not walk alone in life. The readings of the Mass during Advent lift our hopes in the God who responds to our needs. The prophets announced in advance that God would come soon to save us. Every part of the spiritual atmosphere of Advent serves this purpose: to focus on the answer that God gives to our petitions. Jesus Christ our Lord, the Son of God who became man to live among us, is the answer God gives to the prayers we offer to him as we walk our path of life. All that is needed by every person, every family and every community, for us to make straight our steps towards peace and justice is present in the admirable person of the Son of God.

Do we want our children to achieve a better life? Then, they need to get to know Christ personally, so that the light of his Gospel soothes their hearts with virtues of justice, generosity, and zeal to live honestly, so that they do not conform themselves to the greed, self-importance and envy that dominate the world. Do we want to live in a world where the rights of the unborn, the immigrants, and the elderly are respected? Then we must seek the spirit of Christ. He himself tells us: *"What you did for one of these least ones, you did it for me"* (cf. Mt 25: 31-46). If we respond to the grace that invites us to contemplate Christ, (that is to say, if we *lift up our souls*) we will obtain a still deeper grace of courage and strength for the path of life.

St. Paul says in his letter to the Romans 5: 5 *"Hope does not disappoint, because the love of God has been poured out into our hearts through the Holy Spirit that has been given to us."* What is expressed by St. Paul's teachings is the same truth expressed by the psalmist when he says: No one who hopes in you is put to shame. Hope breathes in an atmosphere of love. We do not lose hope because we know, with the certainty of faith, that God loves us. The hope we have in Christ, who came for the first time through the mystery of his Incarnation, continues to grow with the coming of Christ through the grace of the Gospel and the sacraments; and this hope directs our steps as pilgrims walking to meet the Christ who will come at the end of time.

During these days, we have the treasured custom of hanging colorful lights on the trees in our yards, and on the sides of our houses. These are like external signs of welcoming the Child Jesus. At the same time may these lights be living signs of faith, hope, and love, (the brilliant lights of the soul), announcing the Christmas feasts which are drawing near. May you and all your loved ones have a lively love in your hearts in order that you never lose hope in the God who loves us so much. My deep desire is that Advent be for everyone a time of grace to prepare for our Lord Jesus Christ the welcoming that he desires and that he deserves.

Amen.

First Sunday of Advent
November 29, 2020

MARK 13:33-37

Jesus said to his disciples: "Be watchful! Be alert!
You do not know when the time will come.
It is like a man traveling abroad.
He leaves home and places his servants in charge,
each with his own work,
and orders the gatekeeper to be on the watch.
Watch, therefore;
you do not know when the Lord of the house is coming,
whether in the evening, or at midnight,
or at cockcrow, or in the morning.
May he not come suddenly and find you sleeping.
What I say to you, I say to all: 'Watch!'"

 @bpdflores

"The owner of the house entrusts to each one his own work."

If we realize what he has given us, the sense of his handing over and the reason behind his counted steps, then we know that what is given us to do until he comes is the work of one who is loved.

We've been entrusted with the master's domain. We are the gate-keepers on the watch. We know our master's priorities, so when a needy person comes to our door and asks for help, what would the master want us to do? Jesus gives each one of us a wake-up call. A call to love all, especially to love the less fortunate and work tirelessly for their welfare, their human dignity and human rights. Do I respond to this call with all my heart?

_____

_____

_____

_____

_____

_____

_____

_____

_____

_____

_____

_____

_____

_____

_____

Monday of the First Week of Advent

November 30, 2020

Feast of St. Andrew, Apostle

MATTHEW 4:18-22

As Jesus was walking by the Sea of Galilee,
he saw two brothers,
Simon who is called Peter, and his brother Andrew,
casting a net into the sea; they were fishermen.
He said to them,
"Come after me, and I will make you fishers of men."
At once they left their nets and followed him.
He walked along from there and saw two other brothers,
James, the son of Zebedee, and his brother John.
They were in a boat, with their father Zebedee, mending
their nets.
He called them, and immediately they left their boat and
their father and followed him.

 @bpdflores

Mt 4: Jesus said to Simon and Andrew, "Come after me, and
I will make you fishers of men." At once they left their nets
and followed him.

Jesus presents himself to our horizon,
enters our perception, a gust of salty wind or
 a breeze saturated with fresh water; He chooses the way
and suddenly we cannot imagine life without him.

Jesus is constantly calling us and waits for our "YES!" We put Jesus in the mode of Advent. Am I afraid to respond to Jesus's invitation to serve others? What are the blocks that I encounter to say, "I do"? Our baptismal call is our constant reminder.

When the Lord calls, we cannot help but answer. This can seem foolhardy to some. We leave the familiar and trust that the Lord will guide us in learning his way of fishing.

December 1, 2020

LUKE 10:21-24

Jesus rejoiced in the Holy Spirit and said,
"I give you praise, Father, Lord of heaven and earth,
for although you have hidden these things
from the wise and the learned
you have revealed them to the childlike.
Yes, Father, such has been your gracious will.
All things have been handed over to me by my Father.
No one knows who the Son is except the Father,
and who the Father is except the Son
and anyone to whom the Son wishes to reveal him."
Turning to the disciples in private he said,
"Blessed are the eyes that see what you see.
For I say to you,
many prophets and kings desired to see what you see,
but did not see it,
and to hear what you hear, but did not hear it."

 @bpdflores

Although you have hidden these things from the wise
and the learned, you have revealed them to the childlike.*

1 Cor 1, 27:
God chose the foolish of the world to shame the wise,
and God chose the weak of the world to shame the
strong.
It's good to remember where we come from.

Eyes see and ears hear; if I say "tree" you immediately see what you hear, but with the soul, not with the eyes. If I say "the hope of life," go look for Christ with your soul.

A Christian sees more through his ears than with his eyes.

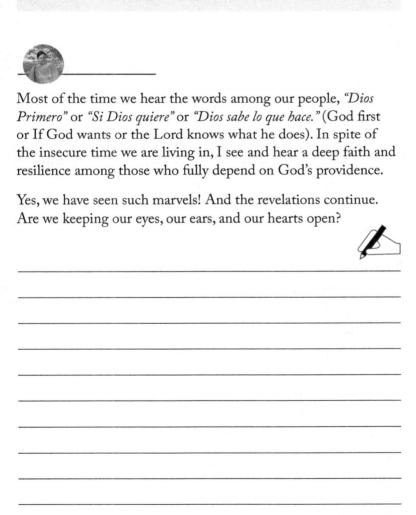

Most of the time we hear the words among our people, *"Dios Primero"* or *"Si Dios quiere"* or *"Dios sabe lo que hace."* (God first or If God wants or the Lord knows what he does). In spite of the insecure time we are living in, I see and hear a deep faith and resilience among those who fully depend on God's providence.

Yes, we have seen such marvels! And the revelations continue. Are we keeping our eyes, our ears, and our hearts open?

_____

_____

_____

_____

_____

_____

_____

_____

_____

_____

_____

December 2, 2020

MATTHEW 15:29-37

At that time:
Jesus walked by the Sea of Galilee,
went up on the mountain, and sat down there.
Great crowds came to him,
having with them the lame, the blind, the deformed, the
mute, and many others.
They placed them at his feet, and he cured them.
The crowds were amazed when they saw the mute speaking,
the deformed made whole, the lame walking,
and the blind able to see,
and they glorified the God of Israel.
Jesus summoned his disciples and said,
"My heart is moved with pity for the crowd,
for they have been with me now for three days
and have nothing to eat.
I do not want to send them away hungry,
for fear they may collapse on the way."
The disciples said to him,
"Where could we ever get enough bread in this deserted
place to satisfy such a crowd?"
Jesus said to them, "How many loaves do you have?"
"Seven," they replied, "and a few fish."
He ordered the crowd to sit down on the ground.
Then he took the seven loaves and the fish,
gave thanks, broke the loaves,
and gave them to the disciples, who in turn gave them to

the crowds.

They all ate and were satisfied.

They picked up the fragments left over – seven baskets full.

 @bpdflores

He gave thanks, broke the loaves, and gave them to the disciples, etc.

The sacramental manifestation of the Lord continues through his giving over "to the disciples, who give to the crowds," that is, his Eucharistic action/presence, given to the Church for the sake of the world.

————

The disciples had brought the few loaves and fishes for themselves: Jesus, blessing and giving, instructs the disciples to give what they have to people whose need is greater.

The loaves multiply when the disciples obey him in faith.

In my interaction with people, I have seen those who have little share easily because they know what it means to be hungry, to be thirsty, to be in need. Do what you can to help those in need. Do not bemoan your insufficiencies, but use your gifts, however small. Hold only with open hands so God's gifts can flow out to others. How are you using your gifts to help those in need?

Jesus who incarnated among us was born poor, without much power and security. His parents were running as refugees to save the life of this little baby. How beautiful to wait in patience to celebrate this baby's birthday.

_____

_____

_____

_____

_____

_____

_____

_____

_____

_____

_____

_____

Thursday of the First Week of Advent

December 3, 2020

Memorial of St. Francis Xavier, Priest

MATTHEW 7:21, 24-27

Jesus said to his disciples:
"Not everyone who says to me, 'Lord, Lord,'
will enter the Kingdom of heaven,
but only the one who does the will of my Father in heaven.
"Everyone who listens to these words of mine and acts on
them will be like a wise man who built his house on rock.
The rain fell, the floods came,
and the winds blew and buffeted the house.
But it did not collapse; it had been set solidly on rock.
And everyone who listens to these words of mine
but does not act on them
will be like a fool who built his house on sand.
The rain fell, the floods came,
and the winds blew and buffeted the house.
And it collapsed and was completely ruined."

 @bpdflores

"Not everyone who says to me, 'Lord, Lord,' will enter the Kingdom of heaven, etc."

"When those who are tending Christ's flock wish that the sheep were theirs rather than his, they stand convicted of loving themselves, not Christ."
(St. Augustine, Treatise on John)

If one receives in his mind the word that Jesus announces, one receives in his soul the Word that Jesus is.

He dwelt among us, conversing with those who drew near, with the purpose of making his dwelling in the soul of each one.

Today we celebrate St. Francis Xavier's feast. His faith was great. He went as a missionary to China and preached the Gospel. He never returned to his homeland.

If our faith is solid as a rock, nothing will shake us. Through the sacraments, we are adopted as sons/daughters of God. Can poverty, natural disasters, injustice and hatred separate us from the love of God? Which rock do we choose to build our lives on? Do we choose the right solid rock and witness to him by our actions?

_____

_____

_____

Friday of the First Week of Advent
December 4, 2020

MATTHEW 9:27-31

As Jesus passed by, two blind men followed him, crying out,
"Son of David, have pity on us!"
When he entered the house,
the blind men approached him and Jesus said to them,
"Do you believe that I can do this?"
"Yes, Lord," they said to him.
Then he touched their eyes and said,
"Let it be done for you according to your faith."
And their eyes were opened.
Jesus warned them sternly,
"See that no one knows about this."
But they went out and spread word of him through all that
land.

 @bpdflores

Let it be done for you according to your faith, etc.

The gaze of Jesus
towards us
is the grace that invites us to faith,
offering us to be able to gaze at him,
not simply in his physical, historical aspect,
but as who he is,
the power of God touching our poverty.

When others cry out for help, is our faith strong as theirs? Is our touching of their lives life-giving, compassionate; is it Christ-like?

The size of the mustard seed of faith is enough for Jesus to save us. The faith of the blind man motivated Jesus to give his sight back to him. Jesus told people who witnessed this healing event to keep quiet about it. He wanted to continue his ministry. But they went out and spread word of him through all that land. Are we aware of all the divine healing in our lives?

Saturday of the First Week of Advent
December 5, 2020

MATTHEW 9:35–10:1, 5A, 6-8

Jesus went around to all the towns and villages,
teaching in their synagogues,
proclaiming the Gospel of the Kingdom,
and curing every disease and illness.
At the sight of the crowds, his heart was moved with pity
for them
because they were troubled and abandoned,
like sheep without a shepherd.
Then he said to his disciples,
"The harvest is abundant but the laborers are few;
so ask the master of the harvest
to send out laborers for his harvest."

Then he summoned his Twelve disciples
and gave them authority over unclean spirits to drive them
out and to cure every disease and every illness.

Jesus sent out these Twelve after instructing them thus,
"Go to the lost sheep of the house of Israel.
As you go, make this proclamation:
'The Kingdom of Heaven is at hand.'
Cure the sick, raise the dead,
cleanse lepers, drive out demons.
Without cost you have received; without cost you are to
give."

 @bpdflores

"Freely you have received."

In the heights of grace, the labor that most makes
us similar to God is to give freely what we most love.
God gave us his Son, and the Son gave us his Mother.
#SanJuanDiego gave what he received.

Jesus definitely wanted God's mission to continue on earth. Jesus
saw the crowds, and his heart was moved with pity for them. He
empowered his disciples and gave them all power to serve the
people. Power is not to boost one's ego but to serve the vulnera-
ble, the least on earth.

Never focus on the cost of discipleship. Cherish this free gift
in your life — and live it generously. You will never run out of
resources, because our God is a generous God.

Advent

Week Two

The Gifts Christ Desires to Give Us

The Lord Jesus wants to give us at least three presents before Christmas even gets here. The thing is, we have to look for them in hidden places. He does not hide them deliberately: rather, given our daily routines, they may as well be hidden.

The first gift he wants to give is a memory to recall him. The Church's 2,000-year experience instructs us that the best way to draw near to Jesus is to practice the cultivation of a graceful memory. Some people are blessed with a naturally good memory. Others, like myself, struggle every morning to remember where we left the car keys the night before. But we can all cultivate a holy memory. How much effort do we put into remembering what Jesus said the last time we picked up the Scriptures and read a passage from the Gospel? The more we try to remember, the more we will remember. This effort bears great fruit. If we call him to mind, he thereby dwells in the mind. Jesus dwells in us by means of his Word, just as the Holy Spirit dwells in us by virtue of charity.

We remember so many unimportant things, like past hurts and what time our favorite televisions shows are on. The memory attains to its noblest purpose, though, when through it we carry the thought of the Lord and his Gospel. Suppose, for example, all you can remember from the Gospel you heard at Mass a few weeks ago is the phrase: *What you did not do for the least of mine, you did not do for me.* That is more than enough to supply for a week's worth of fruitful conversation with the Lord.

But for this to work, we have to be conscious about seeking a quiet place, a string of moments where this Word can stir our thoughts and considerations. Thus the second gift he wants to give us is silence to dwell on his Word. If we want to find silence, the place to look is not so much a place as it is a time. The early morning is best for many; an evening walk is good, too. I recommend meditation before the Blessed Sacrament, but if we cannot make it to church to visit the Sacrament, the remembrance of his presence there can bring us great peace.

The Word emerges from the silence. He speaks from there. And so, for example, remembering the Gospel I mentioned, we can ask him: *Lord, do you want me to be more attentive to your presence in the persons the world considers insignificant?* At this point he no doubt says *yes.* We respond: *But Lord, where can I find you in my daily life?* Be assured he will respond to you. You get the idea. The conversation goes on from there.

Thus, the third gift the Lord wishes to give us during Advent flows from the first two. He wants to give us a grace to recognize and love him. This is the grace that takes what impressions he leaves with us during our prayer and allows them to be enacted in the daily movements of our lives, in the midst of our families, our work, school, recreation. By faith we recognize the presence of Christ. By his Word he points out his presence in our midst. We ask for the grace not only to see him in our daily routine, but to embrace and love him there. To recognize Christ in the world, and to love him there, is not one activity among many in a Christian life; it is the only activity of a Christian life. It is what St. Paul in Galatians 5, 6 *calls that faith that operates through love.*

These three gifts, memory, silence and loving recognition, prepare us to receive the great gift of Christ at Christmas.

We want to be ready for that gift, so that we can better embrace him in love, in the celebration of the Nativity, in the persons with whom we share this life, and in the sacraments through which he shares his life with us.

May God bless you always.

Second Sunday of Advent

December 6, 2020

MARK 1:1-8

The beginning of the gospel of Jesus Christ the Son of God.

As it is written in Isaiah the prophet:
Behold, I am sending my messenger ahead of you;
he will prepare your way.
A voice of one crying out in the desert:
"Prepare the way of the Lord,
make straight his paths."
John the Baptist appeared in the desert
proclaiming a baptism of repentance for the forgiveness of
sins.
People of the whole Judean countryside
and all the inhabitants of Jerusalem
were going out to him
and were being baptized by him in the Jordan River
as they acknowledged their sins.
John was clothed in camel's hair,
with a leather belt around his waist.
He fed on locusts and wild honey.
And this is what he proclaimed:
"One mightier than I is coming after me.
I am not worthy to stoop and loosen the thongs of his
sandals.
I have baptized you with water;
he will baptize you with the Holy Spirit."

 @bpdflores

The Word propelled the preaching of John the Baptist, making us aware that God prepares his own manifestation among us by way of his hidden presence among us: he who is to come is here already.

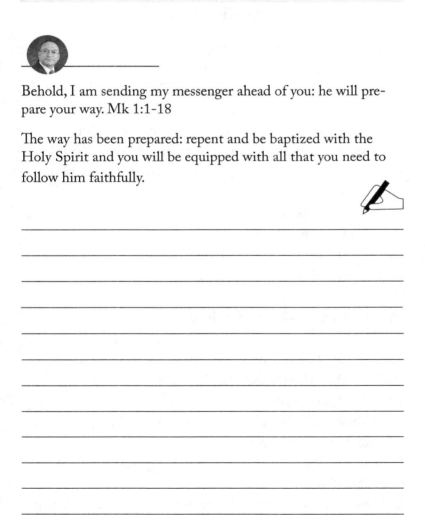

Behold, I am sending my messenger ahead of you: he will prepare your way. Mk 1:1-18

The way has been prepared: repent and be baptized with the Holy Spirit and you will be equipped with all that you need to follow him faithfully.

Monday of the Second Week of Advent
December 7, 2020

*Memorial of St. Ambrose,
Bishop and Doctor of the Church*

LUKE 5:17-26

One day as Jesus was teaching,
Pharisees and teachers of the law,
who had come from every village of Galilee and Judea and
Jerusalem, were sitting there,
and the power of the Lord was with him for healing.
And some men brought on a stretcher a man who was
paralyzed; they were trying to bring him in and set him in
his presence.
But not finding a way to bring him in because of the crowd,
they went up on the roof
and lowered him on the stretcher through the tiles
into the middle in front of Jesus.
When Jesus saw their faith, he said,
"As for you, your sins are forgiven."

Then the scribes and Pharisees began to ask themselves,
"Who is this who speaks blasphemies?
Who but God alone can forgive sins?"
Jesus knew their thoughts and said to them in reply,
"What are you thinking in your hearts?
Which is easier, to say, 'Your sins are forgiven,'
or to say, 'Rise and walk'?
But that you may know that the Son of Man has authority

on earth to forgive sins" –
he said to the one who was paralyzed,
"I say to you, rise, pick up your stretcher, and go home."
He stood up immediately before them,
picked up what he had been lying on,
and went home, glorifying God.
Then astonishment seized them all and they glorified God,
and, struck with awe, they said,
"We have seen incredible things today."

 @bpdflores

Lk 5
"The Son of Man has authority ..."
Authority was redeemed in the person of Jesus: before it
was imprisoned in selfishness; now it is free to receive the
direction of charity, eager to forgive and heal.

————

"They went up on the roof and lowered him on the stretcher."

If we have friends who are animated and capable of taking
us to Jesus when we lack the strength, we are indeed among
the most blessed. Blessed are they for being good, and
blessed are you for having them as friends.

Lk 5:17-26 "Jesus knew their thoughts and said to them in reply, 'What are you thinking in your hearts? Which is easier, to say, 'Your sins are forgiven,' or to say, 'Rise and walk'?"

As the paralyzed man arose when commanded by Our Lord, we too must rise up daily. Jesus lifts us from our daily paralysis of anger, envies, depression, fears and confusion during the most uncertain of times. With him you will see incredible things daily and go on your way always glorifying God!

What are some of the daily paralyses from which you wish to be lifted?

Tuesday of the Second Week of Advent
December 8, 2020

*Solemnity of the Immaculate Conception
of the Blessed Virgin Mary*

LUKE 1:26-38

The angel Gabriel was sent from God
to a town of Galilee called Nazareth,
to a virgin betrothed to a man named Joseph,
of the house of David,
and the virgin's name was Mary.
And coming to her, he said,
"Hail, full of grace! The Lord is with you."
But she was greatly troubled at what was said
and pondered what sort of greeting this might be.
Then the angel said to her,
"Do not be afraid, Mary,
for you have found favor with God.
Behold, you will conceive in your womb and bear a son,
and you shall name him Jesus.
He will be great and will be called Son of the Most High,
and the Lord God will give him the throne of David his
father,
and he will rule over the house of Jacob forever,
and of his Kingdom there will be no end."
But Mary said to the angel,
"How can this be,
since I have no relations with a man?"
And the angel said to her in reply,

"The Holy Spirit will come upon you,
and the power of the Most High will overshadow you.
Therefore the child to be born
will be called holy, the Son of God.
And behold, Elizabeth, your relative,
has also conceived a son in her old age,
and this is the sixth month for her who was called barren;
for nothing will be impossible for God."
Mary said, "Behold, I am the handmaid of the Lord.
May it be done to me according to your word."
Then the angel departed from her.

 @bpdflores

The #ImmaculateConception
"Hail, full of grace":
Grace does not destroy
Grace does not replace
Grace does not take pride
Grace anticipates us
Grace makes it easier for us
Grace makes us able to say "yes" to God

———————

Then the angel said to her: "Do not be afraid, Mary, for you
have found favor with God, etc."

"On your word, O Virgin,
depends comfort for the wretched,
ransom for the captive,
freedom for the condemned, indeed,
salvation for all the children of Adam ..."
–St. Bernard, Abbott

Luke 1: 26-38:
"And coming to her, he said, "Hail, favored one!
The Lord is with you."…

How is the fullness of grace expressed in Mary's soul? As a constant desire to please the Lord. Mary always enjoyed the grace of a burning desire to fulfill what God commanded. To us, poor sinners, grace arrives as a fire to ignite this same desire. When Mary prays for us, she is asking that we have a persisting desire. It is one thing to know the will of God and another to want to fulfill it. May we never lack the desire!

from blog En Pocas Palabras

"The Holy Spirit will come upon you, and the power of the Most High will overshadow you."

Let the Lord overshadow you and the Holy Spirit come upon you and miracles will happen. Believe and do not doubt God's love for you!

Homage to the Virgin

The land had not seen a garden so pristine
nor such a clearly lit stream
since before, it would seem,
that breezy time of the day.*

An Angel had not seen one so splendidly free
nor eyes so suited to light
since before, it would seem,
that breezy time of the day.

And God had not heard so lively a word
nor so light a 'let-it-so-be'
arise from within such an old world
since before, it would seem,
that breezy time of the day.

Reference to Genesis 3:8

Sin Pecado Concebida

Meditación sobre el himno Mística Rosa de intocados pétalos,
(Breviario Romano para el día 8 de diciembre)

Santísima sin pecado concebida
Madre compasiva,
Virgen de inocencia indecible,

Mística Rosa de intocados pétalos,
Tu manto refleja *el límpido cielo de infinitas lámparas,*
Y tus ojos abarcan la condición afligida de tu pueblo.

El Padre y tú pronuncian la misma Palabra:
Dios-Hijo del Padre en el cielo narrado,
Dios-Hijo por ti en tierra cantado,

Santificando primero la morada santa de tu cuerpo,
Tu Hijo *Bajó del cielo*, como dice el Credo,
Abrió así camino que al Padre devuelve.

Por nuestra salvación Dios cruzó la antigua frontera,
Que separa de Dios la criatura expatriada.
Saltó como carnero sobre la vieja muralla.

Musa celeste, cántanos *del Amor-Artífice*,
El Sabio sin tiempo que del Padre procede
Cántanos el sendero que de Él proviene

Muéstranos amar como Él lo quiere,
Sanar las heridas que el odio enciende,
Ser servidores de los relegados
      Entre los cuales Él se esconde.

Cántanos de un futuro luciente
Que solo por Dios se concede.
Y, cuando el viento tu presencia anuncie,
      Pídeme lo que Él requiere. Amen.

Wednesday of the Second Week of Advent
December 9, 2020
Feast of St. Juan Diego

MATTHEW 11:28-30

Jesus said to the crowds:
"Come to me, all you who labor and are burdened,
and I will give you rest.
Take my yoke upon you and learn from me,
for I am meek and humble of heart;
and you will find rest for yourselves.
For my yoke is easy, and my burden light."

 @bpdflores

Mt 11: 28-30
"Come to me, all you who labor and are burdened, etc."

Is 40:30
Though young men faint and grow weary, and youths
stagger and fall, they that hope in the LORD will renew their
strength, will soar as with eagles' wings; they will run and

not grow weary, walk and not grow faint.

"Come to me, all you who labor and are burdened, and I will give you rest."

Unload your heartache, stress, and worries at Jesus' feet so that he will give you rest as he promised. Rest in the immense refuge of his meek and humble heart, his Sacred Heart, burning with unquenchable fire for love of you. From what do you need rest?

_____

_____

_____

_____

_____

_____

_____

_____

_____

_____

_____

_____

_____

_____

_____

_____

_____

Thursday of the Second Week of Advent
December 10, 2020

MATTHEW 11:11-15

Jesus said to the crowds:
"Amen, I say to you,
among those born of women
there has been none greater than John the Baptist;
yet the least in the Kingdom of heaven is greater than he.
From the days of John the Baptist until now,
the Kingdom of Heaven suffers violence,
and the violent are taking it by force.
All the prophets and the law prophesied up to the time of John.
And if you are willing to accept it,
he is Elijah, the one who is to come.
Whoever has ears ought to hear."

 @bpdflores

Mt 11:11-15
"Amen, I say to you, among those born of women there has
been none greater than John the Baptist; yet the least in
the Kingdom of heaven is greater than he."

Because with the coming of Christ and his work of
redemption the rivers of grace have been unleashed.

Mt 11:11-156 "The Kingdom of heaven suffers violence, and the violent are taking it by force."

Rise up and defend the Kingdom of Heaven, for our Savior will come soon and hold us accountable for our actions and inactions. What actions is God calling you to?

_____

_____

_____

_____

_____

_____

_____

_____

_____

_____

_____

_____

_____

_____

_____

_____

_____

_____

_____

Friday of the Second Week of Advent
December 11, 2020

MATTHEW 11:16-19

Jesus said to the crowds:
"To what shall I compare this generation?
It is like children who sit in marketplaces and call to one another,
'We played the flute for you, but you did not dance,
we sang a dirge but you did not mourn.'
For John came neither eating nor drinking, and they said,
'He is possessed by a demon.'
The Son of Man came eating and drinking and they said,
'Look, he is a glutton and a drunkard,
a friend of tax collectors and sinners.'
But wisdom is vindicated by her works."

 @bpdflores

Mt 11:16-19
We played the flute for you, but you did not dance, we sang a dirge but you did not mourn.*

Sometimes we are contrary for the pure enjoyment of being contrary. And this has to frustrate the Lord very much.

Mt 11:15-19 "The Son of Man came eating and drinking and they said, 'Look, he is a glutton and a drunkard, a friend of tax collectors and sinners.'"

Be a glutton and drunkard in the Lord our Savior, always seeking what pleases him and serves his kingdom. Critics will always have a comment if you follow Jesus, so give them something to talk about. Their conversion may depend on it!

How are you seeking what pleases the Lord our Savior?

_____

_____

_____

_____

_____

_____

_____

_____

_____

_____

_____

_____

_____

_____

_____

Saturday of the Second Week of Advent
December 12, 2020
Feast of Our Lady of Guadalupe

LUKE 1:39-47

Mary set out
and traveled to the hill country in haste
to a town of Judah,
where she entered the house of Zechariah
and greeted Elizabeth.
When Elizabeth heard Mary's greeting,
the infant leaped in her womb,
and Elizabeth, filled with the Holy Spirit,
cried out in a loud voice and said,
"Most blessed are you among women,
and blessed is the fruit of your womb.
And how does this happen to me,
that the mother of my Lord should come to me?
For at the moment the sound of your greeting
reached my ears, the infant in my womb leaped for joy.
Blessed are you who believed
that what was spoken to you by the Lord
would be fulfilled."
And Mary said:
"My soul proclaims the greatness of the Lord;
my spirit rejoices in God my savior."

 @bpdflores

Who am I that the mother of my Lord should come to me?

The presence of Mary in person, Mother of the Word Incarnate, announces the Gospel of the God who draws near, of the Hope that does not fail, of the Dawn breaking from on high, of the Christ who comes dispersing the darkness.

———

Lk 1, 43: And how does this happen to me, that the mother of my Lord should come to me?

Zec 2, 14: See, I am coming to dwell among you, says the LORD. Many nations shall join themselves to the LORD on that day, and they shall be his people, and he will dwell among you.

———

Elizabeth cried out: "Most blessed are you among women, etc."

Oh WORD so great that you reduced yourself to our condition while remaining the divine spring of all blessing. Your eternity dwelt for 9 months in the womb of Mary, who for our cause was the first and the most blessed.

"And how does this happen to me, that the mother of my Lord should come to me?"

As Elizabeth, we should also say, "And how does this happen to me, that the mother of my Lord should come to me?" She comes to aid us during the Rosary with understanding. Being the mother of our Lord, she has the special communication of motherly compassion for all of us.

Our Lady of Guadalupe:
A Gentle Voice Announcing

These are intense days of devotion and prayer in the United States, and certainly here in the Rio Grande Valley. On December 8, we celebrate the Immaculate Conception, Patronal Feast of our Cathedral here in the Diocese of Brownsville, and since 1847, patroness of the United States. And yet four days later, on December 12 we celebrate the great feast of Our Lady of Guadalupe, Patroness of the Americas. The two feasts are deeply connected in the mystery of faith. On December 8, we recall the truth that God chooses to give the full gift of grace on his own initiative, to prepare Mary from the first moment of her conception for her mission. On December 12, we are given a vivid reminder of what that mission entails. The Virgin's presence announces that the Lord is coming to be with his people, to free us from death, darkness and sin.

On December 12, I wish I could be everywhere at once in the Rio Grande Valley; the processions, the Masses in all the parishes, in small mission chapels, and at the Basilica; *las Mañanitas*, the menudo and *hojarascas* — it's everywhere. And it is for everyone: families, the elderly, small children in costumes; laughing, singing, high school students playing in mariachi bands, fireworks. It is joyous, reverent and a full display of the mystery of faith alive in our land. This feast is a singular grace for our diocese and our nation, worthy of a special place in the hearts of all Catholics in the United States.

There are so many reasons for this exuberance. And yet in the end they are all one simple reason keenly felt by all of us who celebrate her day. The Virgin, in her very person, because her person bears the Son of God, appears in 1531 as the gentle voice announcing to a good but labored soul that heaven is kind and very close, and that the darkness will not have its way forever. There was much blood spilled in the Americas both prior to the arrival of the Spanish Empire, and after. Human sacrifice gave way to a conquest that was in many ways brutal. It was hard in those days to believe in the triumph of light over darkness, mercy over vengeance, reconciliation over recrimination. But somehow, in the Virgin's appearing, in the image of the innocent one already bearing the Son of God in her womb, the announcement of mercy went forth and was joyfully received.

This is the cause of our joy: God has appeared in our land; he has taken flesh from the Virgin; and we need not fear that the darkness will in the end prevail. She comes as the breeze that announces that the springtime of the human race is possible by the grace of God's favor. The Gospel brings this springtime, and for us in the Americas, Our Lady left us the Gospel written as an image on Juan Diego's tilma. The Gospel was the hope of the peoples of the Americas when the Virgin appeared, and it is the hope of our future as a people. There is urgent need for this hope. We in the Valley know too well that much blood is spilled senselessly for power, greed, vengeance, and drugs. A new sort of cult of death menaces our children. Our Lady of Guadalupe and the Christ she bears forth to our world show us the way out of this encroaching despair.

Perhaps it is time to designate Our Lady of Guadalupe as Co-patroness of the United States. Together with the Immaculate Conception on December 8, and Our Lady of Guadalupe on December 12, we could as Catholics in the United States renew our appreciation for the way grace works in us by contemplating the Mother of God under these two magnificent invocations. For us also, grace is given by God's wise design to both make us holy, and to send us forth to announce that the long reign of sin is ending. The one follows upon the other. There is no evangelization without holiness; and grace is given so as to be shared with a world that dwells in darkness and under the shadow of death.

Our Lady conceived without sin, pray for us that no sin impede our reception of your Son into our lives!

Our Lady of Guadalupe, pray that having received him, we be worthy bearers of your Son to others!

Saludo a la Virgen:
Inmaculada y Guadalupe

Luz inmaculada
por el Padre fuiste intencionada
como sonrisa de niñita
en el Verbo imaginada,
y fuego tierno de anuncio
desde el principio anticipada.
Si la lucidez angélica fue
la primera por Dios creada
(como Agustín en sus libros
con frecuencia comentaba),
esa belleza tan alta
ni Adán recién plasmado
hubiera con sus ojos claros
alcanzado mirar.
Porque en luces sin espacios
él no se podía fijar,
(como Tomás el angélico
más tarde dirá.)
Sin embargo el Padre
ya guardaba en su seno
hermosura más alta
para sus hijos ajenos.
Creación singular
esperando su día,
la rayita mas pura,
lo que tu vida será.
Nuestra eres,

carne y hueso,
llena de gracia
y mas clara por eso,
humilde morena,
sencilla nobleza,
honor singular de nuestra raza
de mezclada naturaleza.
El Verbo saltó
al poderte encontrar,
en tal belleza inventada
para nuestros ojos contemplar.
Al oír tu reflexión
en su ser pronunciada
regocijó de antemano
que de ti a su creación
Él podría llegar.
El Espíritu ardía
por querer verte aparecer,
como aurora amanecida,
lo que ni ángeles podrán comprender.
En la llegada de tu día,
anuncio de la más excelente instauración,
te saludamos, hermanita,
de quien Dios quiso nacer.
Eres la Llama inocente
dando luz a los pueblos
llamados en ti
a recibir la mañana,
y a tu Hijo conocer.
Amen.

Advent

Week Three

This Advent Meditate on Lines
From the Baptismal Creed

During these days before we celebrate the Nativity of the Lord, I recommend meditation on the last lines of the baptismal Creed. The Creed is the ancient summary of the Apostles' preaching and the teachings of the New Testament. And the last phrases lead us into a future that is born in us through God's Son, born of the Virgin Mary by the work of the Holy Spirit.

> I believe in the Holy Spirit,
> the holy Catholic Church,
> the communion of saints,
> the forgiveness of sins,
> the resurrection of the body
> and life everlasting.

We believe in the Holy Spirit: In fact, the Holy Spirit is revealed to the world by his works. We profess our faith in the third person of the Holy Trinity precisely because the arrival of Jesus, the Son of God in person, is the same moment of the revelation of the Holy Spirit in person. Through the Holy Spirit, the Son comes to live what is ours. And Jesus, God made man and glorified, sends us the plenitude of the Holy Spirit. The mystery of the Pentecost is still actual. The Church professes faith in the Holy Spirit because she knows him as the author and sustainer of her life.

We could say that the last phrases of the Creed announce the last works of the Holy Spirit. Some of them occur today; others are to come.

The profession of faith of the Holy Catholic Church is the profession of the presence, according to God's design, of the one Holy, Catholic Church. She is holy by the power and grace of the Holy Spirit. Not in a sense that there is no sin among her members, but in the sense that only through the grace of the Gospel announced by the Church, and the sacraments shared by the Church, sinners hope to become saints. This means that the Holy Church is an extension of Christ himself in the world. Holiness looks for us, and were it not for the historical and concrete presence of the Church constituted by the Gospel and the sacraments, none of us would have hope to share the heritage of God's Kingdom. We must believe in the Church; which means to believe within the Church and to believe in the Church as an instrument of the Incarnate Word, established as the sacrament of his presence and his work in the world.

Then we profess faith in the communion of saints. This refers to the unity of the Church formed by members from heaven and earth. It includes all the members of the Church who are awaiting total purification in Purgatory. We all belong to the same ecclesial body, all united by bonds of the grace of Christ, the head of the Church. Nevertheless, the Church here on earth keeps fighting with weapons of grace against the powers that desire to destroy the work of God. The Book of Revelation speaks of this. In addition, although the history of the Church includes stories of great sinners from the beginning (for example, the one who betrayed Jesus), we also profess that there has never been a lack of extraordinary triumphs of grace over evil. From the first Apostles, the martyrs throughout history, to the saints of our time, such as Mother Teresa of Calcutta, or Blessed Miguel Pro or the recently beatified Carlo Acutis, the Church is constituted to give birth to and nourish saints.

We believe in the forgiveness of sins: To profess the communion of saints means the Church continues being a fruitful Mother, and through the sacrament of Baptism, new members become part of the Church with all their sins forgiven. An essential part of the mission of the Church is to announce that there is forgiveness for everyone who humbly repents from their sins and asks for the mercy of God, which has been fully manifested in Jesus Christ, who died and rose to gain for us this forgiveness. In addition, it is only by finding God's forgiveness that we can learn how to forgive one another. And the truth is that it is a requirement for those who want to share eternal life, that they learn how to forgive others.

We believe in the Resurrection of the flesh and in eternal life: In the history of the Church, martyrs overcame cruel death precisely because of the grace of the Holy Spirit, sustaining them in faith in the resurrection of the flesh and in eternal life. We may say that the last phrases of the Creed are inscribed on the flesh of the martyrs. Devotion to the martyrs is an instruction in the faith of the Church, especially in our faith in the world to come. Martyrs teach us that God's love made manifest in Christ is knowing how to die so that we can live.

The work of Jesus and the work of the Holy Spirit is a work aiming to reconcile the entire universe with God our Father. The Holy Spirit inspires us and moves us internally to seek the Kingdom of Jesus in our lives. If we pay attention to the Holy Spirit, we will seek the grace of Christ in the Gospel and in the sacraments of the Church. And this prepares us to receive the Lord at the end of our personal life, and at the end of the history of the world.

Christ will come again to present us to the Father. We will rise in our own flesh. And just as we are, flesh and soul, we will receive the judgment of a fair and compassionate judge. The possibility of finally losing our life, that is, losing entrance to the eternal life of the saints, does exist. God judges and it is not like we do not know what he will ask us at the end. But the Church lives, prays and gives herself in order that all can be saved. We remember, then, that God was born of a Virgin in Bethlehem to open this dark world to the grace of our being able to be numbered in the communion of saints, in the eternal banquet of the beloved Son.

Amen.

Third Sunday of Advent
December 13, 2020

JOHN 1:6-8, 19-28

A man named John was sent from God.
He came for testimony, to testify to the light,
so that all might believe through him.
He was not the light,
but came to testify to the light.

And this is the testimony of John.
When the Jews from Jerusalem sent priests
and Levites to him
to ask him, "Who are you?"
He admitted and did not deny it,
but admitted, "I am not the Christ."
So they asked him,
"What are you then? Are you Elijah?"
And he said, "I am not."
"Are you the Prophet?"
He answered, "No."
So they said to him,
"Who are you, so we can give an answer to those
who sent us?
What do you have to say for yourself?"
He said:
"I am *the voice of one crying out in the desert,
'make straight the way of the Lord,'*"
as Isaiah the prophet said."
Some Pharisees were also sent.

They asked him,
"Why then do you baptize
if you are not the Christ or Elijah or the Prophet?"
John answered them,
"I baptize with water;
but there is one among you whom you do not recognize,
the one who is coming after me,
whose sandal strap I am not worthy to untie."
This happened in Bethany across the Jordan,
where John was baptizing.

 @bpdflores

John the Baptist affirmed: I am not the Christ*

Pointing to the presence of Christ in the world requires
that we reflect more than ourselves, something beyond the
possibilities already present in the world. A mirror reflects
the light that comes from outside, or it is darkness.

J ohn the Baptist came before Jesus not
O nly to testify to the light but
H e also came to be the voice of Christ even
N ow – today

How do I testify to the light of Christ today?

In what situation am I being called to be "the voice of Christ" today?

_____

_____

_____

_____

_____

_____

_____

_____

_____

_____

_____

_____

_____

_____

_____

St. John the Baptist Bearing Witness

Monday of the Third Week of Advent
December 14, 2020

MATTHEW 21:23-27

When Jesus had come into the temple area,
the chief priests and the elders of the people approached
him as he was teaching and said,
"By what authority are you doing these things?
And who gave you this authority?"
Jesus said to them in reply,
"I shall ask you one question, and if you answer it for me,
then I shall tell you by what authority I do these things.
Where was John's baptism from?
Was it of heavenly or of human origin?"
They discussed this among themselves and said,
"If we say 'Of heavenly origin,' he will say to us,
'Then why did you not believe him?'
But if we say, 'Of human origin,' we fear the crowd,
for they all regard John as a prophet."
So they said to Jesus in reply, "We do not know."
He himself said to them,
"Neither shall I tell you by what authority I do these
things."

 @bpdflores

"By what authority do you do these things?" Mt 11, 19

Wisdom is vindicated by her works. "Everything he did and everything he said on earth ... was actually you speaking to us in your Son, appealing to us by your love and stirring up our love for you." -William of St. Thierry

A uthority – God gives
U s his Authority
T o teach
H is word
O r to
R espond to his
I nvitation
T o follow Jesus who lives among us
Y esterday, today, and always.

How do I teach his word or respond to his invitation today?

_____

_____

_____

_____

_____

_____

_____

Tuesday of the Third Week of Advent

December 15, 2020

MATTHEW 21:28-32

Jesus said to the chief priests and the elders of the people:
"What is your opinion?
A man had two sons.
He came to the first and said,
'Son, go out and work in the vineyard today.'
The son said in reply, 'I will not,'
but afterwards he changed his mind and went.
The man came to the other son and gave the same order.
He said in reply, 'Yes, sir,' but did not go.
Which of the two did his father's will?"
They answered, "The first."
Jesus said to them, "Amen, I say to you,
tax collectors and prostitutes
are entering the Kingdom of God before you.
When John came to you in the way of righteousness,
you did not believe him;
but tax collectors and prostitutes did.
Yet even when you saw that,
you did not later change your minds and believe him."

 @bpdflores

If we do not seek the grace of ever deeper repentance,
neither are we seeking how to receive Christ.

V ineyard can be the world you and
I traverse daily with a
N ew opportunity
E ach day to respond; to say
Y es – but not only say "yes" like the first son
A nd not do anything; but say "yes" and
R espond like the second son
D id.

What did I do today that God called me to do?

_____

_____

_____

_____

_____

_____

_____

_____

_____

_____

_____

_____

_____

_____

_____

Wednesday of the Third Week of Advent
December 16, 2020

LUKE 7:18B-23

At that time,
John summoned two of his disciples and sent them
to the Lord to ask,
"Are you the one who is to come, or should we look for
another?"
When the men came to the Lord, they said,
"John the Baptist has sent us to you to ask,
'Are you the one who is to come, or should we look for
another?'"
At that time Jesus cured many of their diseases,
sufferings, and evil spirits;
he also granted sight to many who were blind.
And Jesus said to them in reply,
"Go and tell John what you have seen and heard:
the blind regain their sight, the lame walk, lepers are
cleansed, the deaf hear, the dead are raised,
the poor have the good news proclaimed to them.
And blessed is the one who takes no offense at me."

 @bpdflores

Lk7,19f: "Tell John: the blind see [...] and the poor have
the gospel preached to them."

The Lord's work announces his identity.

Does ours?

C ured: We are the blind, the lame, the deaf, the
U s, because Jesus came to
R edeem us and proclaim the Good News to
E veryone. All of us are broken in some way and are cured whether we
D eserve it or not.

How does the Good News of Jesus cure me of my brokenness?

_____

_____

_____

_____

_____

_____

_____

_____

_____

_____

_____

_____

_____

_____

_____

December 17, 2020

MATTHEW 1:1-17

The book of the genealogy of Jesus Christ,
the son of David, the son of Abraham.
Abraham became the father of Isaac,
Isaac the father of Jacob,
Jacob the father of Judah and his brothers.
Judah became the father of Perez and Zerah,
whose mother was Tamar.
Perez became the father of Hezron,
Hezron the father of Ram,
Ram the father of Amminadab.
Amminadab became the father of Nahshon,
Nahshon the father of Salmon,
Salmon the father of Boaz,
whose mother was Rahab.
Boaz became the father of Obed,
whose mother was Ruth.
Obed became the father of Jesse,
Jesse the father of David the king.
David became the father of Solomon,
whose mother had been the wife of Uriah.
Solomon became the father of Rehoboam,
Rehoboam the father of Abijah,
Abijah the father of Asaph.
Asaph became the father of Jehoshaphat,
Jehoshaphat the father of Joram,
Joram the father of Uzziah.

Uzziah became the father of Jotham,
Jotham the father of Ahaz,
Ahaz the father of Hezekiah.
Hezekiah became the father of Manasseh,
Manasseh the father of Amos,
Amos the father of Josiah.
Josiah became the father of Jechoniah and his brothers
at the time of the Babylonian exile.
After the Babylonian exile,
Jechoniah became the father of Shealtiel,
Shealtiel the father of Zerubbabel,
Zerubbabel the father of Abiud.
Abiud became the father of Eliakim,
Eliakim the father of Azor,
Azor the father of Zadok.
Zadok became the father of Achim,
Achim the father of Eliud,
Eliud the father of Eleazar.
Eleazar became the father of Matthan,
Matthan the father of Jacob,
Jacob the father of Joseph, the husband of Mary.
Of her was born Jesus who is called the Christ.
Thus the total number of generations
from Abraham to David
is fourteen generations;
from David to the Babylonian exile, fourteen generations;
from the Babylonian exile to the Christ,
fourteen generations.

 @bpdflores

"God stepped into history. When the eternal Son became man, He did so in reality, without protection or exception, vulnerable by word and act; woven, like us, into the stifling web of effects that proceed from the confused hearts of men."

—Romano Guardini

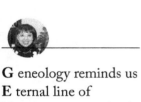

G eneology reminds us that we are part of an

E ternal line of

N ew generations built upon

E ach preceding one. Not

O nly is there a

L ineage of 14 generations from David to the Babylonian Exile and not

O nly are there 14

G enerations from the Babylonian Exile to Christ, but

Y ou and I are part of Christ's lineage because we are His disciples.

How have I been a disciple of Jesus Christ today?

_____

_____

_____

_____

Friday of the Third Week of Advent
December 18, 2020

MATTHEW 1:18-25

This is how the birth of Jesus Christ came about.
When his mother Mary was betrothed to Joseph,
but before they lived together,
she was found with child through the Holy Spirit.
Joseph her husband, since he was a righteous man,
yet unwilling to expose her to shame,
decided to divorce her quietly.
Such was his intention when, behold,
the angel of the Lord appeared to him in a dream and said,
"Joseph, son of David,
do not be afraid to take Mary your wife into your home.
For it is through the Holy Spirit
that this child has been conceived in her.
She will bear a son and you are to name him Jesus,
because he will save his people from their sins."
All this took place to fulfill
what the Lord had said through the prophet:
Behold, the virgin shall be with child and bear a son,
and they shall name him Emmanuel,
which means "God is with us."
When Joseph awoke,
he did as the angel of the Lord had commanded him
and took his wife into his home.
He had no relations with her until she bore a son,
and he named him Jesus.

 @bpdflores

St. Joseph in relation to Mary and the angel of his dreams illuminates the profound meaning of the words of St. Paul (1 Cor 13, 7): "Love believes all things, hopes all things, endures all things."

"He was a righteous man": God's justice lived within St. Joseph, the pre-eminent grace of his vocation, and an anticipated participation of the fullness of justice in the soul of Christ.

"Joseph her husband, since he was a righteous man, etc." When the God of justice and understanding enters into a world that lacks both justice and understanding, he chooses and raises up in grace a just and understanding man to protect his vulnerable entrance.

Matthew 1: 1-25: "Joseph, son of David, do not be afraid to take Mary your wife into your home. For it is through the Holy Spirit that this child has been conceived in her." ... Mary received the Mystery of Incarnation with humble faith, unbreakable hope, and intense love. Everything started with the dialog between her and the angel. With the help of the angel visiting the dreams of St. Joseph, Mary was able to communicate to Joseph the mystery to which he would devote his life, the protection of the Virgin and her son. Joseph received the message with firm faith in God, and with trust in Mary. As a just man, he fulfilled his mission with courage and without complaints. From heaven the remarkable mystery of the Incarnation arrived to Mary's heart and body, and it arrived through Mary and the angel to the life of St. Joseph. May we receive the annunciation with Joseph's firm faith and with Mary's joy!

from blog En Pocas Palabras

J ust as Joseph
O pened his heart to the
S urprising news of the
E ternal Word wrapped in Mary's
P regnant body, may we open our
H earts this season to the Good News of Our Lord Jesus.

How am I preparing today to receive this incredible Good News that "God is with us"?

_____

_____

_____

_____

_____

_____

_____

_____

_____

_____

_____

_____

_____

Saturday of the Third Week of Advent
December 19, 2020

LUKE 1:5-25

In the days of Herod, King of Judea,
there was a priest named Zechariah
of the priestly division of Abijah;
his wife was from the daughters of Aaron,
and her name was Elizabeth.
Both were righteous in the eyes of God,
observing all the commandments
and ordinances of the Lord blamelessly.
But they had no child, because Elizabeth was barren
and both were advanced in years.
Once when he was serving as priest
in his division's turn before God,
according to the practice of the priestly service,
he was chosen by lot
to enter the sanctuary of the Lord to burn incense.
Then, when the whole assembly of the people was praying
outside
at the hour of the incense offering,
the angel of the Lord appeared to him,
standing at the right of the altar of incense.
Zechariah was troubled by what he saw, and fear came
upon him.
But the angel said to him, "Do not be afraid, Zechariah,
because your prayer has been heard.
Your wife Elizabeth will bear you a son,
and you shall name him John.

And you will have joy and gladness,
and many will rejoice at his birth,
for he will be great in the sight of the Lord.
He will drink neither wine nor strong drink.
He will be filled with the Holy Spirit even from his mother's womb,
and he will turn many of the children of Israel
to the Lord their God.
He will go before him in the spirit and power of Elijah
to turn the hearts of fathers toward children
and the disobedient to the understanding of the righteous,
to prepare a people fit for the Lord."
Then Zechariah said to the angel,
"How shall I know this?
For I am an old man, and my wife is advanced in years."
And the angel said to him in reply,
"I am Gabriel, who stand before God.
I was sent to speak to you and to announce to you this good news.
But now you will be speechless and unable to talk
until the day these things take place,
because you did not believe my words,
which will be fulfilled at their proper time."
Meanwhile the people were waiting for Zechariah
and were amazed that he stayed so long in the sanctuary.
But when he came out, he was unable to speak to them,
and they realized that he had seen a vision in the sanctuary.
He was gesturing to them but remained mute.
Then, when his days of ministry were completed, he went home.
After this time his wife Elizabeth conceived,

and she went into seclusion for five months, saying,
"So has the Lord done for me at a time when he has seen fit
to take away my disgrace before others."

 @bpdflores

As if the angel were saying: If you cannot glorify God for
what will be fulfilled, better silence until you can sing what
he has done.

———

The Forerunner will "turn the hearts of fathers toward
children": A grace that fathers do not fully realize they
need until their hearts are in fact turned.

———

"God will go before him in the spirit and power of Elijah ...
to prepare a people fit for the Lord."

A people fit; that is to say,
a people patiently disposed to perceive the deeds and
designs of the Lord in our midst.
Above the noise,
within the time,
beneath the waves.

———

LK 1: 5-25
"You will be speechless and unable to talk until the day
these things take place, etc."

Just as the child does not speak if he does not first hear
what his mother says, in the Kingdom, to speak is a
response to, and depends on, having received with faith
the Word that comes from above.

G abriel, the
A ngel of the Lord,
B rought
R ejoicing news to Zechariah, as he lit the
I ncense, that his barren wife
E lizabeth would bear a son named John destined to prepare a
people for the
L ord.

How do I help my family prepare for the coming of the Lord today?

_____

_____

_____

_____

_____

_____

_____

_____

_____

_____

_____

_____

_____

Advent

Week Four

How Advent Turns Into Christmas

I tend to live Advent as an intense experience of feeling like time is running out. Most concretely this happens when I realize I want to get thoughtful presents for my nieces and nephews. I have a few weeks. But the time runs out, so I end up depending on Amazon expedited shipping to get me out of a jam. How superficial, you say! Maybe, but giving a gift is noble in itself, and rightly a Christmas thing; yet we postpone the opportunities. On another level, (speaking analogously and in a theological sense), I know I am supposed to prepare in some way to be able to celebrate the mysteries of Christmas.

Christmas is like the liturgical roadblock that reminds us we have to recover the heart of a child in order to know Jesus and enter into his Kingdom. And every year I find myself facing the approach of the 25th wishing that Christian insight and simplicity of heart could come by expedited shipping. I should have meditated the Gospel more, spent more time with the Blessed Sacrament, been more conscious of ways to help the poor. Time runs out, though, and the liturgical roadblock starts looking like a vehicle heading in my direction. Jesus is coming again. I am not just heading to meet him. He is moving towards me. I sense him coming from afar. Time is a gift. Don't let it slip away.

The 25th arrives like someone knocking at the door. We knew that a visitor was coming, but the knock always comes as a kind of surprise. It takes on the aspect of a day of judgment. Ouch! Time ran out.

The change starts simply, the whisper of grace rising through nature. Christmas ascends from beyond us and is offered to each of us. *Do you see what I see? Said the night wind to the little lamb. Do you see what I see?* The simple innocence of his coming finds welcome in the poor and lowly: *Said the little lamb to the shepherd boy, do you hear what I hear?* From the lowly the sound is amplified to reach the mighty king: *Said the shepherd boy to the mighty king, do you know what I know?* This grace insinuates itself smoothly first as something seen, then as a sound heard, until reaching to become something known. Or, better yet, something savored.

He does not come in the way we had thought. When he comes, it is something simple. When all is said and done, not everything depended on my pressured preparations. There is joy, the kind you cannot plan on. The hand of glory comes by way of the fingered blessing of a child.

In the gentleness of the descent of the Word Incarnate, he takes on the aspect of a challenge. *A Child, a Child shivers in the cold.* In this posture, the child becomes a sword, just like when he becomes a sword on that Friday of the Cross. The only sword that the Christ sought to brandish was the one that could penetrate to our deepest heart, making us able to feel something of compassion again. The showing invites a response. By becoming a small child like any of us, he makes us able to receive his piercing appeal, and respond to him.

Do we see? Can we begin to understand? The child who is God shivers. He makes himself the vulnerable one, capable of being welcomed or rejected, embraced or struck, remembered or forgotten. Can we go to him? A shepherd brings the message to us. Can we heed him? *In your palace warm, mighty king?* There is still hope that our stony hearts can be converted into hearts of flesh. It all begins with the presence of the God made flesh and blood. In the manger, on the Cross, he looks for an opening into the interior of each one of us.

We talk a lot about the hope that is born on Christmas. I think that there is a risk that we will accept hopes of coal because we fail to recognize the real treasure that this child brings us. It all has to do with the appeal he makes to us. The human heart will never be as close to its hopes than when it sees this child asking for recognition and compassion, in the name of every human being that has entered into the world. God became more human than any of us. By becoming man, God embraced all that we are; he did not reject us.

The first grace, carried by the night wind, is his coming in our flesh. The grace that follows is the response that we give him in every human being that we encounter today. This is the only way that we have to embrace this child. What a marvel! We have hopes of becoming more like God with a simple response made to the child who is God. Kissing his feet, we say to him: Make me, O Lord, as human as you. There we encounter our hope.

Sunday of the Fourth Week of Advent
December 20, 2020

LUKE 1:26-38

The angel Gabriel was sent from God
to a town of Galilee called Nazareth,
to a virgin betrothed to a man named Joseph,
of the house of David,
and the virgin's name was Mary.
And coming to her, he said,
"Hail, full of grace! The Lord is with you."
But she was greatly troubled at what was said
and pondered what sort of greeting this might be.
Then the angel said to her,
"Do not be afraid, Mary,
for you have found favor with God.
"Behold, you will conceive in your womb and bear a son,
and you shall name him Jesus.
He will be great and will be called Son of the Most High,
and the Lord God will give him the throne of David his
father,
and he will rule over the house of Jacob forever,
and of his kingdom there will be no end."
But Mary said to the angel,
"How can this be,
since I have no relations with a man?"
And the angel said to her in reply,
"The Holy Spirit will come upon you,
and the power of the Most High will overshadow you.

Therefore the child to be born
will be called holy, the Son of God.
And behold, Elizabeth, your relative,
has also conceived a son in her old age,
and this is the sixth month for her who was called barren;
for nothing will be impossible for God."
Mary said, "Behold, I am the handmaid of the Lord.
May it be done to me according to your word."
Then the angel departed from her.

 @bpdflores

Then the angel said to her: "Do not be afraid, Mary, for you
have found favor with God, etc."

"On your word, O Virgin, depends comfort for the wretched,
ransom for the captive, freedom for the condemned,
indeed, salvation for all the children of Adam ..."

–St. Bernard, Abbott

My Lord, this is it … the time has come for you to fulfill the promise reiterated to your people over the centuries. And you have chosen to make it so in the peaceful silence of the womb of the Blessed Virgin of Nazareth. Through her humble docility, you chose to become one with us in our human nature in time, so that we could become one with you in your divine nature in eternity.

Lord Jesus, show me where in my heart I still resist your will, so that by your grace I may yield to your desire for me.

Monday of the Fourth Week of Advent
December 21, 2020

LUKE 1:39-45

Mary set out in those days
and traveled to the hill country in haste
to a town of Judah,
where she entered the house of Zechariah
and greeted Elizabeth.
When Elizabeth heard Mary's greeting,
the infant leaped in her womb,
and Elizabeth, filled with the Holy Spirit,
cried out in a loud voice and said,
"Most blessed are you among women,
and blessed is the fruit of your womb.
And how does this happen to me,
that the mother of my Lord should come to me?
For at the moment the sound of your greeting reached my
ears, the infant in my womb leaped for joy.
Blessed are you who believed
that what was spoken to you by the Lord
would be fulfilled."

 @bpdflores

Elizabeth cried out: "Most blessed are you among women,
etc."

Oh WORD so great that you reduced yourself to our
condition while remaining the divine spring of all blessing.
Your eternity dwelt for 9 months in the womb of Mary, who
for our cause was the first and the most blessed.

Mother Mary, you bore your Creator, the Eternal Word in your womb for nine months, yet you were always blessed, for he was ever in your heart after. Teach me to lovingly bear him in my own heart, that his Presence within me may bring joy and hope to everyone that I meet.

Tuesday of the Fourth Week of Advent
December 22, 2020

LUKE 1:46-56

Mary said:
"My soul proclaims the greatness of the Lord;
my spirit rejoices in God my savior.
for he has looked upon his lowly servant.
From this day all generations will call me blessed:
the Almighty has done great things for me,
and holy is his Name.
He has mercy on those who fear him
in every generation.
He has shown the strength of his arm,
and has scattered the proud in their conceit.
He has cast down the mighty from their thrones
and has lifted up the lowly.
He has filled the hungry with good things,
and the rich he has sent away empty.
He has come to the help of his servant Israel
for he remembered his promise of mercy,
the promise he made to our fathers,
to Abraham and his children for ever."
Mary remained with Elizabeth about three months
and then returned to her home.

 @bpdflores

The Church learns from Mary how to sing to God:

It is not just a question of knowing the words, but of being
conformed to the God we sing.

———

"Those who refuse to be humbled cannot be
saved. They cannot say with the prophet: See,
God comes to my aid; the Lord is the helper of my
soul. But anyone who makes himself humble like
a little child is greater in the kingdom of heaven."
—Bede the Venerable

———

"From this day all generations will call me blessed ..."
To be able to greet Mary,
to share wholeheartedly in her joy
for the singular grace she receives from the Most High,
is to be able to participate with her
in the work of the Holy Spirit
by which the Son enters the world.

O Blessed Mother, your soul proclaimed the greatest song of praise ever written, and you sang it at every moment. Though I am weak and imperfect, wounded by my own sins and the sins of others, help me to grant him access to my heart, that confessing my sins, I may praise his mercy, and recognizing his hand in all things, I may proclaim his goodness.

_____

_____

_____

_____

_____

_____

_____

_____

_____

_____

_____

_____

_____

_____

_____

Wednesday of the Fourth Week of Advent
December 23, 2020

LUKE 1:57-66

When the time arrived for Elizabeth to have her child
she gave birth to a son.
Her neighbors and relatives heard
that the Lord had shown his great mercy toward her,
and they rejoiced with her.
When they came on the eighth day to circumcise the child,
they were going to call him Zechariah after his father,
but his mother said in reply,
"No. He will be called John."
But they answered her,
"There is no one among your relatives who has this name."
So they made signs, asking his father what he wished him
to be called.
He asked for a tablet and wrote, "John is his name,"
and all were amazed.
Immediately his mouth was opened, his tongue freed,
and he spoke blessing God.
Then fear came upon all their neighbors,
    and all these matters were discussed
throughout the hill country of Judea.
All who heard these things took them to heart, saying,
"What, then, will this child be?
For surely the hand of the Lord was with him."

 @bpdflores

"His tongue was freed":

Human speech is in a certain sense stuck in a mire until the moment we realize that God has directed a word to us: the grace of being able to respond to him is a liberation of the tongue.

Lk 1:57-66
Zechariah asked for a tablet and wrote, "John is his name, etc."

The last word left written by the prophets was the name of the one who was going to point out by his life and death how all the prophetic words converge in Christ.

Time and again, Father, you have done the impossible and fulfilled your promises to your people. All you require is that I choose to believe and to do your will, even when things don't seem to make sense; only in that do we experience the glorious freedom of the children of God. Grant me your peace as I await the fulfillment of your word, in your time, so that I may praise you even as I wait.

December 24, 2020

Christmas Eve Mass in the Morning

LUKE 1:67-79

Zechariah his father, filled with the Holy Spirit,
prophesied, saying:
"Blessed be the Lord, the God of Israel;
for he has come to his people and set them free.
He has raised up for us a mighty Savior,
born of the house of his servant David.
Through his prophets he promised of old
that he would save us from our enemies,
from the hands of all who hate us.
He promised to show mercy to our fathers
and to remember his holy covenant.
This was the oath he swore to our father Abraham:
to set us free from the hand of our enemies,
free to worship him without fear,
holy and righteous in his sight
all the days of our life.
You, my child, shall be called the prophet of the Most High,
for you will go before the Lord to prepare his way,
to give his people knowledge of salvation
by the forgiveness of their sins.
In the tender compassion of our God
the dawn from on high shall break upon us,
to shine on those who dwell in darkness and the shadow of
death, and to guide our feet into the way of peace."

 @bpdflores

Lk1: "Blessed be the Lord, the God of Israel; for he has visited and redeemed his people."

God's visit becomes redemption when he is welcomed.

_____

"The dawn from on high shall break upon us, to shine on those who dwell in darkness and the shadow of death." The God made man arrives as the dawn from on high so that men might know that to be humanized in truth is to accept to be transfigured by grace.

Lord, you are so close — at every moment, but especially now, in this sacred moment. With great anticipation during this season of Advent, we have longed for this holy night. Help us to make whatever final preparations are necessary to give your Son, the Radiant Dawn, a worthy welcome when he comes.

O good St. Joseph, your love and devotion made the humblest of mangers fit for the Lord of lords. Stay with us, that together we may render fitting praise to the newborn King at his birth.

_____

_____

_____

_____

_____

The Nativity of the Lord
December 25, 2020
Christmas Midnight Mass

LUKE 2:1-14

In those days a decree went out from Caesar Augustus
that the whole world should be enrolled.
This was the first enrollment,
when Quirinius was governor of Syria.
So all went to be enrolled, each to his own town.
And Joseph too went up from Galilee from the town of
Nazareth to Judea, to the city of David that is called Beth-
lehem, because he was of the house and family of David,
to be enrolled with Mary, his betrothed, who was with
child.
While they were there, the time came for her to have her
child, and she gave birth to her firstborn son.
She wrapped him in swaddling clothes and laid him in a
manger, because there was no room for them in the inn.
Now there were shepherds in that region living in the fields
and keeping the night watch over their flock.
The angel of the Lord appeared to them
and the glory of the Lord shone around them,
and they were struck with great fear.
The angel said to them,
"Do not be afraid; for behold, I proclaim to you good news
of great joy that will be for all the people.
For today in the city of David a savior has been born for
you who is Christ and Lord. And this will be a sign for you:

you will find an infant wrapped in swaddling clothes and lying in a manger."

And suddenly there was a multitude of the heavenly host with the angel, praising God and saying:

"Glory to God in the highest and on earth peace to those on whom his favor rests."

 @bpdflores

Luke 2:1-14: "There were shepherds in that region living in the fields and keeping the night watch over their flock."
...

Shepherds took care of the sheep, and witnessed the angel's presence. All creation is present in this scene. The Child Jesus brings peace precisely because in his person God has come close to the world of the human beings. The closeness of God is the salvation of man because it opens a way of communion between heaven and earth. But we must take the offered path! The shepherds took the road to Jesus to receive the salvation that had come close through Mary's son. We must give this testimony of the closeness of God and the path that leads to life. This testimony is the cause of joy for the angels.

The Adoration of the Shepherds

And a Child Shall Guide Them

Christmas falls on us at the appointed time, interrupting the course of our plans and activities. We knew that it was coming, but we put it off or decided to ignore it. We had much to do; lots of running around and little time to lose.

"Yes, son, maybe tomorrow we will go to see the Christmas lights on all the houses."

"No, Mom, I won't forget to get a Christmas present for my aunt. Don't worry; I still have time to do it."

"Mom, do you have the mailing address for my cousin? I don't think I will have time to go by my aunt's house."

The television interrupts its usual programming and without wanting to, the reporters show us images of violence. Words fail us. What a tragedy! They were innocent children. We see tears and inconsolable families.

"Oh, Lord, what can we do?"

Spontaneously, we think of the children. And during the days that follow, we hug each one a little tighter, and for a little longer. And maybe we feel a little guilty: I should do this every day. Life is precious, and vulnerable. And there are many things in life we do not understand.

"May God help us."

We frantically run from one thing to another, like people looking for a buried treasure; small preoccupations consume us, and so do divisions and arguments that do not make much sense in the long run. Time passes. Our children grow up.

"When did you get so tall?"

We are mysterious and vulnerable creatures. We easily forget that we already possess the treasure. If the ray of light does not fall to us from the heavens, we stay in a state of forgetting and of darkness, unable really to see what we have in front of our eyes.

The 25th arrives. We ran out of time. It falls on us brusquely. Can't do much about that, it's here.

"Come now, son, we are going to go see the Nativity scene after Mass."

"How pretty it is."

"Mom, there are lots of people around."

"That's right, but in a little while we will be able to get closer."

"Dad, what are we looking at?"

"It is the child Jesus. God became a little child, son, just like you and your little sister were not too long ago. The child is cold, but he is happy; he has his family around him."

"And why did God enter the world in the winter when it was cold?"

"Well, I am not sure, son, maybe it was to give to Mary and Joseph the joy of being able to snuggle him close to warm him. And maybe it was so he could warm the home of Mary and Joseph with his divine love."

Christmas is a light that penetrates through the clouds, and it reaches to the most obscure corners of life to heal us of our forgetfulness and our blindness. We already have the treasure we were looking for. We are not alone. Yes, there is much to do, but not like we had previously thought. We have children to embrace, and old folks to kiss. We have friends with whom to carry our burdens and with whom to enjoy life; and we have family members to console, and with whom to rejoice. Life is precious and it is vulnerable, a gift without price. My brother needs me, and I need him in my life. Together we can make it.

"Merry Christmas, son, and thanks very much for stopping by.

"Same to you, Auntie. May you have a very happy day."

"Say hello to your mother for me. May God protect you." A kiss, a more conscious hug, lasting a bit longer.

It was for this that the great God made himself small. The love of God is the pathway toward our love for one another. We do have much to do; love is on the march, but the shadows do not dispel without resistance. Eyes of faith see that the light that falls from heaven has the face of a child; he is the leader that goes before us on our path. As was foretold by the prophet Isaiah: "A little child shall guide them."

Happy Christmas-tide to everyone. May the Lord God who became man grant you light to see, and love to envelop your homes this Christmas, and every day of your lives.

Notes about the tweets/reflections

- In the tweets, the use of "etc." is a personal bow to the way St. Thomas Aquinas cited scripture. St. Thomas, like most medieval commentators on Scripture, considered that people were familiar with the rest of the passage.

- Dates of the original posts have been removed so as not to distract from the reflections.

Artwork Used

Cover
Garofalo (Benvenuto Tisi), *Annunciazione,* 1528, Musei Capitolini, Rome, Italy.

p. 6
Nicolas Poussin, *The Annunciation*, circa 1655–1657, National Gallery, London, England.

p. 17
Stained glass window of the Visitation, Georgetown Visitation Monastery, Washington, D.C.

p.41
Francisco Rizi, *The Dream of St. Joseph,* ca. 1665, Indianapolis Museum of Art, Indianapolis, Indiana.

p. 57
Bartolome Esteban Murillo, *The Assumption of the Virgin,* 1670, Hermitage Museum, St. Petersburg, Russia.

p. 75
Baltasar del Aguila, *Anunciación del Ángel a María,* 1560, Museum of Fine Arts of Córdoba, Córdoba, Spain.

p.84
Annibale Carracci. *St. John the Baptist Bearing Witness*, ca. 1600, The Metropolitan Museum of Art, New York.

p. 105, 128
Bartolome Esteban Murillo, *The Adoration of the Shepherds*, circa 1650, Colección Real (colección Florencio Kelly), Palacio Real Nuevo, Madrid, Spain.

CPSIA information can be obtained
at www.ICGtesting.com
Printed in the USA
LVHW051112241120
672558LV00004B/394